To our wonderful kids:

Joshua
Nicholas
Max
Russell
Gwynnie
Flora

And, of course, our amazing illustrator, Caroline.

And to the children of the Coronavirus Pandemic everywhere.

THE INSANELY AWESOME PANDEMIC PLAYBOOK

A Humorous Mental Health Guide For Kids

Elizabeth Englander, PhD
Katharine Covino, EdD
Illustrated by Caroline Charland

ISBN-10: 9798579585493

Cover design by: Caroline Charland
Printed in the United States of America

CONTENTS

PREFACE

For parents and teachers, and especially for parents who are currently (and
perhaps, temporarily) their children's
teachers, look soon for a companion
guide:

*The Pandemic Playbook for
Parents and Teachers*

The Insanely Awesome Pandemic Playbook:

A Humorous Mental Health Guide for Kids

By

Elizabeth Englander, PhD

Katharine Covino, EdD

Illustrated by Caroline Charland

introduction

Ok, so things are a little different and weird these days.

Ok - a *lot* different! School's different. Friends are different. Your parents are different, too. Those scamps are crazier than they ever were before.

Chances are you may be feeling a little different yourself. The way life is right now is probably not what you were expecting and likely not what you're used to...

Take birthday parties on Zoom, for example. Even though it's great to see your friends, even though that Escape Room is pretty nifty, and even though it is cool to all be able to watch a movie - it's just not the same somehow.

I think everyone could universally agree that hitting a piñata is much (MUCH) more fun in person. Pinning the tail on the donkey gets a bit harder over Zoom as well. And don't get me started on Trick or Treating online. Is Santa Claus supposed to show up on Zoom this year?

But - and it's a BIG BUTT - *we're all adapting.* You probably saw your friends in the last few weeks! You might even be back at school! And we bet that your parents are getting used to working at home. So, gradually, things are moving in the right direction.

Remember how we all used to run around shrieking in the morning, trying to get out the door to school and work? Remember how often you forgot your lunch, your homework folder, or your gym bag? Remember that one time when your mom forgot you at play practice? Well, for a lot of us, things are calmer now. And that's not a bad thing.

That's kind of what this book is about. It's an *Insanely Awesome* way to help you and your family adapt to the new world we are all living in right now. "Covid Times" won't last forever. Someday, everything will go back to almost how it was (and you'll get forgotten at play practice all over again).

But for right now, *The Insanely Awesome Pandemic Playbook* can help you figure out a thing or two. You get a chance to think about family, friends, school, screens, and activities (and there might be some *choice* fart jokes along the way!).

CHAPTER ONE

it's time for school - online school, that is....

Let's talk about *distraction, organization,* and *bombing.* Yes! Bombing! But don't just skip ahead to that section.

ALL ABOUT Distraction

Maybe you feel like as soon as you try to focus on schoolwork, something more interesting pops up in your brain to distract you. Whether it's checking out the latest Minecraft video on YouTube, "borrowing" a piece of your sister's Halloween candy, or sneaking off to play with a new pet bird - it can be impossible to concentrate.

It's like that time, a million years ago, when you were dreamily looking out of the window at school, and the teacher had to call your name THREE TIMES before you jumped!

To: Pre-pandemic Self   Details

iMessage with Pandemic Self
Today, 8:24 PM

Wow! I had forgotten about that time! Super Embarrassing... 😳

Let's not talk about it... 😣

But that's what's happening every day now. It's really hard to focus on school work. 📚

How so?

Well, I sit down at the kitchen table with my laptop. 💻 and my little brother runs around behind me, yelling and whacking things with his foam pool noodle! Meanwhile, Mom is usually on a Zoom call with her boss. It is SO NOISY - Every.Day. I even dream about that pool noodle! 😫

Delivered

Yeah, actually that does sound kind of obnoxious... 🙄

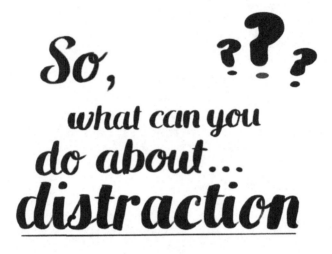

So, ??? what can you do about... distraction

Let's talk about WHERE you get your school work done. We know, we know - super sore subject, right? Your parents ordered your spiffy new desk in August - AUGUST - **AUGUST!** - and still no sign it's coming any time this year.

So, please, put that tragedy out of your mind for just a second. Let's talk about places to work that are not currently **"lost in the mail."**

Some kids like to work in their rooms. Your room can be a good choice if you're able to work independently without being distracted (by Minecraft, stolen candy, or pet birds named Han Solo).

15

But sometimes folks can feel disconnected and isolated in their rooms all day. So your room, even though it has all your favorite stuffed animals that you would never admit to loving, may not be the right place for you.

Other kids like to do school work downstairs - maybe in the family room, or even at the kitchen table. These spaces work really well for those who are ok with a bit more noise and distraction - in terms of other people.

If it doesn't bother you that your mother listens to NPR while she's folding laundry, that your father slams the pans as he's washing them, and that your brother talks in a baby voice to the dog, then downstairs or the kitchen might be just the ticket.

If your mom speaks Spanish, for example, doing your Spanish homework where she can help out would be *muy bueno*....if you take our meaning.

The important thing to know is that **preferences about where you work are very personal.** Meaning that everyone will feel comfortable and productive in different places. Sometimes, even the

same person will prefer different places for different types of work.

Try different locales - see what works for you! There's a fine line between being isolated on a lonely, barren island (your room) and distracted by the tumult of the crowd (the kitchen table). Bottom line - try it and see for yourself!

You can also look around for distractions you can TURN OFF. Turn off the TV and the radio; you can even put away other devices, like your cell phone. Yes! It's possible to put away your cell phone!

The Cell Phone Bounty Hunters won't immediately pounce on your phone and turn it in for a hefty reward!

Fewer distractions mean you can *relax* and concentrate more easily.

All About
organization

One stratagem (boy, does that sound like a super-smart British chess player, or what?) is to try and get organized with your school work. When your mom

asks you to organize your room or organize your desk, your first thought might be that you'd rather be dropping an anchor on your toe, right?

So, ??? *what can you do about... organization* ???

We hear you. But organizing your school materials, your notebooks, your print outs, and even your HUGE box of stuff for gym class (why you need six different colored scarves for gym we'll never know) can help you find what you need when you need it.

FUNNY FILL-INS

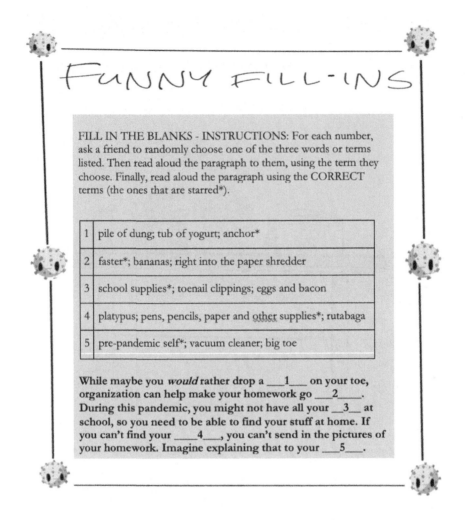

FILL IN THE BLANKS - INSTRUCTIONS: For each number, ask a friend to randomly choose one of the three words or terms listed. Then read aloud the paragraph to them, using the term they choose. Finally, read aloud the paragraph using the CORRECT terms (the ones that are starred*).

1	pile of dung; tub of yogurt; anchor*
2	faster*; bananas; right into the paper shredder
3	school supplies*; toenail clippings; eggs and bacon
4	platypus; pens, pencils, paper and other supplies*; rutabaga
5	pre-pandemic self*; vacuum cleaner; big toe

While maybe you *would* rather drop a ___1___ on your toe, organization can help make your homework go ___2___. During this pandemic, you might not have all your __3__ at school, so you need to be able to find your stuff at home. If you can't find your ___4___, you can't send in the pictures of your homework. Imagine explaining that to your ___5___.

ALL ABOUT
Zoom Bombing

Ok, so parents are not perfect, and likely yours are a little stressed out right now. And they want to help you. They don't want you to fall behind in school.

You might be a little surprised to hear that they can also - sometimes - actually be a distraction while you're at school online, just as they're trying to help you out.

Your parents! Ha! We know, we know - there's lots that your parents do that seems helpful. They set up your work-station, they print your materials, and they find all that crazy stuff you need for remote gym class (seven nine-inch circles, each of a different shade of con-struction paper...really?...REALLY?!).

But what if - while trying to be helpful - they *Zoom Bomb* your class?

● ● ●

To: Pre-pandemic Self   Details

iMessage with Pandemic Self
Today, 9:28 PM

Ok, school on a computer. I'm with you so far. So what's Zoom Bombing?

Ok, so you know how you are looking at the laptop and your teacher is there and he asks you a question?

No. Sounds weird.. 😜

It is, sort of. Anyway....He asks me to answer a question and sometimes my Dad will pass me a note with the answer or whisper it to me!!

He's telling you the answers..while you're in school?! Cool!! 😎

It might sound cool, but it's just another distraction. Plus it makes my teacher nuts! 😫 And it's super embarrassing 😳 It makes me look like a dummy!

Delivered

iMessage   😃 ᫂

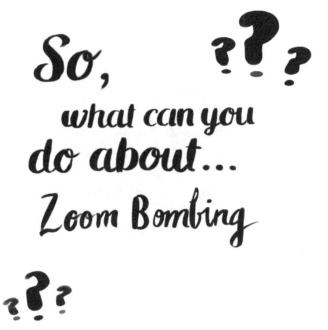

So, what can you do about... Zoom Bombing

The first thing to do is to try to be understanding. Sometimes parents just can't help themselves. In an effort to be supportive, they are just TOO SUPPORTIVE. In an effort to stay involved, they are just TOO INVOLVED. Which is kind of both a good thing and a bad thing for kids in school.

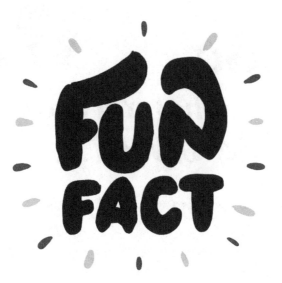

Imagine, for a minute, if your shoelaces were just a tad too supportive. Shoelaces! Awesome, right? Sometimes they are stylish. Sometimes they glow in the dark. But most important of all, they keep your shoes on your feet! Now, imagine if you have shoe laces for your Skechers that went all the way up to your undercarriage. A good idea in theory, perhaps.

You can't be too careful with keeping your shoes on your feet.

But in reality, if shoelaces went all the way up your legs, at some point, maybe mid-calf, you would probably find them more distracting than helpful. Parents being overly involved in your Zoom classes are just like those shoelaces.

Wonderful, and indeed, necessary, up to a point. But past that point, they're totally distracting (and sometimes also uncomfortable).

So, if you don't like tag-teaming long division with your dad, you can politely remind him that you've got this! Plus, because he grew up in the Dark Ages (long before the Common Core), let's be honest, it's also highly likely he has no idea how to do it anyway.

CHAPTER TWO

screens, screens, and more screens....

D o you feel zombified from too much tech?   Do you find that spending too much time with your new best friend (READ - your iPad) makes your eyes cross? Come on now, be honest. We all know that dull-eyed look that happens when we've been staring at a screen for far too long.

It makes you feel like staggering down the middle of your street, groaning and moaning, with your arms stretched out in front of you.

IPAD..

Wouldn't *that* freak out elderly Mrs. Doddery! Maybe you look something like that?

Or....maybe you look like a hypnotized monkey? An inebriated sea slug?

In any event, no matter how the look strikes you, we all know that a moment comes when you absolutely cannot, under any circumstances, look at a screen for another millisecond.

Or maybe...worst of all...you *never* really feel that way!

All About

screens, sleep, and eyes

just an aside

You know how we were all already doing too many screens before the pandemic? Well, a survey in April found that since the pandemic has started, screen time for most kids has doubled on average.

That's a *lot* of screen time.

Some screen time is good. Fine. A-Okay. But, even the best, most wonderful things - when DOUBLED - become somewhat terrifying. Let's take french fries. Everyone loves french fries. People who say they don't are just plain lying. Old people, young people, heck, even vegans love French Fries.

But, what if we told you that everytime

you sat down to eat french fries, you'd have to eat DOUBLE what you usually do? Imagine you couldn't leave the table until your DOUBLED portion of french fries were all gone-o. All of a sudden those fries would look less like a delicious fried gift, and more of a greasy, fried burden.

Same thing with screens...doubling screen time can turn a *good* thing into a *not-so*-good thing.

So, ??? what can you do about... Too many screens? ???

At the moment you feel that screened-out feeling (or, indeed, slightly before it strikes), plan on spending some time away from screens. Do something non-screen-related. We know it's tempting to think that once you're done with your math assignment you can take a break by playing Minecraft. We understand the temptation. Really, we do! We want to work on the iron farm just as much as the next person.

But one potential drawback of staring at a screen until your eyes cross is that your eyes might actually get cross with you. (You see what we did there…? Ha!) Your eyes are used to receiving and processing natural light.

Too much unfiltered blue light – like the kind that comes out of TVs, phones, and computer monitors - can cause all kinds of symptoms, from eye tiredness, to eye strain, to double vision, to headaches. Your eyes aren't used to staring at the bright light of screens all day. Doing it too much exhausts them.

Imagine for a second that one day you were forced to wear ankle weights when you played soccer. Don't ask us why - maybe it was the curse of an evil sorcerer, maybe you just had a very strange soccer coach - who knows...

You could do it, right? You could play soccer even with weights around your ankles. You could probably do it for a while. But pretty soon you would notice that your legs, ankles, and shins would start getting tired - more tired than when you usually play.

Looking at a computer screen asks your eyes to do more work, and different work, than they're used to doing. It's like putting teeny, tiny weights on your eyeballs and then asking them to weight-lift.

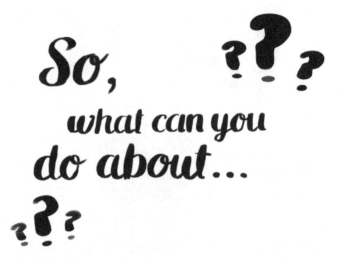

So, what can you do about...

the effect of screens on your eyes

Fortunately, there are some things you can do to help out the only set of eyeballs you'll ever own. First, you can take breaks. Even looking up at something other than a screen - the leaves falling outside, your sister outside on the swing, or your brother tripping as he drags the trash cans up the driveway - would give your eyeballs a well-deserved break.

Also, you can plan your day so that you build in screen breaks. After your language arts class on Zoom, you could plan to make slime, relax in the tub, play on the zipline, or put plastic wrap over the toilet seat so your mom experiences the full evil effects of your humor - any of these worthy pursuits would give the old eyeballs a break.

For the more fashion-forward among us, there are special glasses you can wear that block out the blue light and help prevent eye strain. Besides helping your eyes take a break, they can make you look extremely hard-working and intelligent.

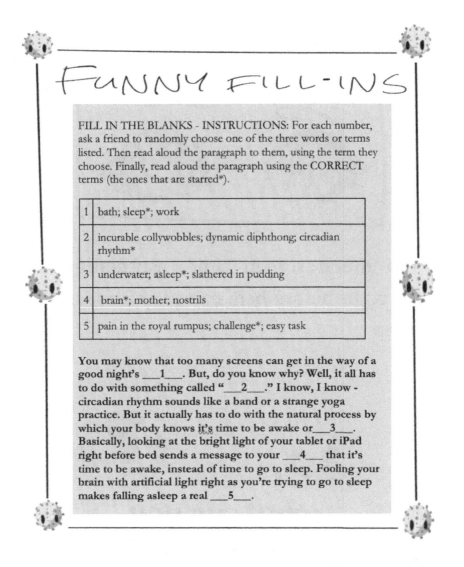

FUNNY FILL-INS

FILL IN THE BLANKS - INSTRUCTIONS: For each number, ask a friend to randomly choose one of the three words or terms listed. Then read aloud the paragraph to them, using the term they choose. Finally, read aloud the paragraph using the CORRECT terms (the ones that are starred*).

1	bath; sleep*; work
2	incurable collywobbles; dynamic diphthong; circadian rhythm*
3	underwater; asleep*; slathered in pudding
4	brain*; mother; nostrils
5	pain in the royal rumpus; challenge*; easy task

You may know that too many screens can get in the way of a good night's ___1___. But, do you know why? Well, it all has to do with something called "___2___." I know, I know - circadian rhythm sounds like a band or a strange yoga practice. But it actually has to do with the natural process by which your body knows it's time to be awake or___3___. Basically, looking at the bright light of your tablet or iPad right before bed sends a message to your ___4___ that it's time to be awake, instead of time to go to sleep. Fooling your brain with artificial light right as you're trying to go to sleep makes falling asleep a real ___5___.

It's not just your eyes that can suffer from too many screens, though - your sleep can also start to short-circuit.

That's right.

Too much screen time, especially if it's right before bed, can interfere with sleep.

When you stare at a bright screen right before sleep, your poor brain gets a little confuzzled, and has a harder time switching into sleep mode. Bottom line - you sometimes end up taking longer to fall asleep or you don't sleep as well.

You might want to think about other things to do right before falling asleep. Maybe plotting how to steal more candy, maybe writing in your diary about your secret crush, or maybe even reading a plain, old-fashioned book. Anyway, your brain and your eyes will thank you!

It turns out, though, that there are other problems with watching too many screens, apart from the eyes and the sleep.

Another problem that can pop up is FOMO. For those who don't know what FOMO is, it's an initialism that stands for... Friendly Ogres Munching Olives? No. Let's see. Four Ordained Man-sized Ostriches? That doesn't sound right. Is it Foul Odors Manufactured Oboes?

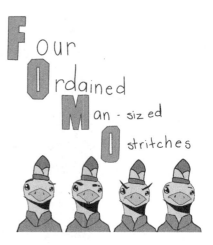

Wrong again. Ha! Yes! This is it! FOMO stands for FEAR OF MISSING OUT.

To: Pre-pandemic Self   Details

iMessage with Pandemic Self
Today, 3:24 PM

Fear Of Missing Out has ALWAYS been a thing. Even in the "Before Times" it would stink 😠 when I would see pictures of Hannah and Claire at a sleepover ｚᶻ 🎉 that I wasn't invited to...

But now, FOMO can seem even worse! 😣 See, right now, decisions about activities during Covid can vary from family to family..

You mean that some families do stuff like parties, when other families don't? 😬

Well, big parties are pretty much gone, but some people can have small parties...it depends on who's in their family and how risky it is for them 😷

Delivered

Wow, I can see how that could be frustrating 😤 to see pictures and posts 📰 of people who are doing things that your family can't do..

● ● ●

iMessage   😀 ⑪⑪

So, ???
what can you
do about...
FOMO?
???

Don't get us wrong, we mean, if your family has decided that soccer is out for the season, it's hard to see your friends playing soccer. It just is. FOMO - or feeling left out, excluded, and lonely - is real and it just stinks. And not in a good way, like a horse barn or a barbeque restaurant. It stinks like old trash, moldy lasagna, and gnarly swimming-pool Bandaids that you see at the bottom and then pop up again in someone's hair. You get the idea.

To avoid the stink of FOMO, try to plan activities, outings, and treats that your social circle feels comfortable doing. Activities that don't involve a screen actually do the best job at taking the piquant stank out of a bad case of FOMO.

You get the idea. In general, it's important to spend time away from screens! So, let's think about some things that we can do when we're taking a "Screen Break."

We thought that phrase would be cool

and would remind us all of "Spring Break!" But then we remembered, Spring Break was cancelled last year and might be cancelled this year as well. Thanks a lot, Covid. Sheesh.

◆ ◆ ◆

Maybe you could have a snack or a meal? You must be hungry (even after all that illicit Halloween candy). Maybe you could cook with your big brother? We know, his repertoire is mostly egg-related, but it could still be fun! Maybe you could go outside with your sister? Walk the dog with your grandma? Milk the cows with your uncle? Wash the car with your great-aunt? Build a rocket-ship for lunar exploration with your granddad?

In terms of helping you feel better, the *person* is usually more important than the *activity*. Maybe you don't really like milking the cows, but doing things with your favorite uncle probably always makes you feel good.

◆ ◆ ◆

Whatever activity you choose - from the ordinary to the extraordinary - it's important to get a break from screens and hopefully go outside! Remember, there's no such thing as bad weather, just bad clothes. Find your galoshes, wrap yourself up warmly, and dress for success!

CHAPTER THREE
why we still have to leave the house...occasionally

S ome things that happen to you are like water off a duck's back, but other things can leave a mark, at least for a little while. Remember when you had the ingenious idea of drawing a luxuriant mustache on your sister's face with a permanent marker?

Remember how your mom flipped out when it didn't come off? And your sister (your poor sister) just had to wait for a week until it wore off? Ha! Now that was a special time.

Some of the things that are happening to people during this pandemic are kind of like that permanent marker. They're going to leave a mark, for a while, but over time, they're probably going to wear off.

What's more, you don't have to just sit around and suffer - there are things you can do to feel better! (Like your sister: she really could have enjoyed that mustache a bit more while she had it...)

Three things that can sometimes leave a temporary mark - like that Sharpie mustache - are *stress, boredom,* and *isolation.*

ALL ABOUT

STRESS!!

Have you ever tried to make a beautiful color by mixing paints? You start with some red, then add a little orange. Then, to make it more original, you think maybe some purple would be the way to go. Very quickly, however, you realize your mistake when your hand-mixed color turns to …. well… couleur de caca as the French would say…

Stress is sort of like that brown glop. It's a feeling you get that's a combination of different stuff, like maybe a little bit of worry, and a little bit of pressure because there's something you're supposed to do, and a little bit of I-don't-like-this. Stress is like getting a splinter - it happens to everyone, and it's definitely no fun, but boy, don't you feel great when it's pulled out of your knee!

FUNNY FILL-INS

FILL IN THE BLANKS - INSTRUCTIONS: For each number, ask a friend to randomly choose one of the three words or terms listed. Then read aloud the paragraph to them, using the term they choose. Finally, read aloud the paragraph using the CORRECT terms (the ones that are starred*).

1	academic*; romantic; intergalactic
2	unappetizing; titillating; boring*
3	chain letter; virus*; juicy rumor
4	jobs*; pants; hair pieces
5	nose picking; belly dancing; worrying*

It's been hard to concentrate on ___1___ stuff lately. I know, I know - it's always been hard to concentrate on school because sometimes school is just super ___2___. But no. Now, it's different. Now, it's stressful. There's a ___3___ circulating. People are losing their ___4___. It's hard not to constantly be ___5___. All that stress makes it impossible to focus.

So, ???
what can you
do about...
???
STRESS!!

Dealing with stress means sometimes being nicer to yourself and allowing yourself a piece of your sister's hard-earned Halloween candy. It means practicing things that help you relax. Have you ever tried yoga?

Maybe you have a parent who'd like to learn it with you! Or maybe curling up on the sofa with a good book works for you, or going for a walk outside. Did you know that walking outside can actually lower your blood pressure? Try to recognize any symptoms of stress, like having a shorter attention span than a goldfish. Stress isn't a disease. It's something we're all experiencing now, and having some symptoms of stress is normal.

Just like diarrhea. Sometimes, we all have diarrhea. It's normal, it's natural. But like stress, you'd probably want to get your symptoms under control.

Quickly. Real soon. Definitely before the rope climb in gym class...

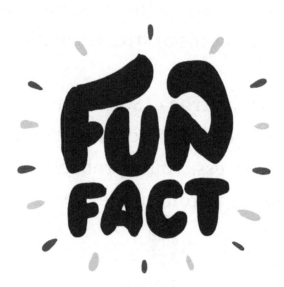

Walking outside, even for just 10 minutes, can help relieve stress, anxiety, and depression. So, bundle up and get out there!

◆ ◆ ◆

ALL ABOUT

SOCIAL
ISOLATION

Advice about staying safe during the Covid-19 pandemic is everywhere, right? A lot of it has to do with social distancing. The distance that everyone tells you to stand apart is six feet. How long is six feet? Great question!

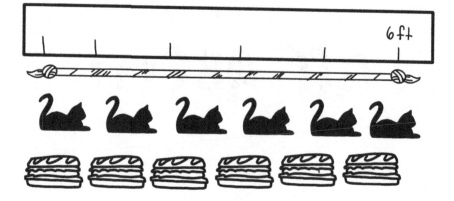

Six feet is the height of a slightly tall man, a pretty tall woman, or a freakishly tall child. Six feet is the length of a dog leash. Six feet is the length of a MacBook charger. You get the idea...

So, ??? what can you do about... ???

SOCIAL ISOLATION

Even if 6 feet seems too far apart, don't despair! There are plenty of things you can do when you're six feet from someone. You can talk, do crafts, eat, sing, play volleyball, golf, sled down a hill, walk on a beach, sit around a campfire, or watch a movie.

The really cool thing about all the activities we just listed is that they can also ALL BE DONE OUTSIDE. While we don't know everything about how Covid-19 spreads, experts do agree that *outside* is safer than *inside.*

Sometimes it's even possible to take an activity that usually happens inside - painting, for example - and move it outside. *Et voilà!* You are both artistic and safe!

The important thing is that SOCIAL DIS-TANCE does not equal SOCIAL ISOLA-TION. It's important to still see your family, friends, teachers, coaches, and youth group leaders. It just might look a little different and take a little more effort than it did before.

Challenge!

Read through these activities. While admittedly ALL of them are ridiculous - some are safer than others.

Which do you think are safe? Which are unsafe? How do you know?

ACTIVITY	SAFE or UNSAFE?
Giving your cousin the traditional "bite on the ear" when he comes to visit for the first time in 6 months.	
Using a megaphone to describe the state of your untrimmed toenails to the folks putting on a golf course green.	
Waiting until your dad is relaxing in his favorite chair, and then throwing rotten apples at the side of the house for three hours.	
Taking a walk with someone while using your pet Python as a six-foot measuring tape to stay an appropriate distance apart.	
Doing a chest bump with everyone at soccer.	
Sneaking up on people just as they're about to lick their ice cream cone and yelling, "SURPRISE!"	
Playing Laser Tag with your teachers on a warm Sunday evening.	

Unsafe, safe, safe, unsafe, unsafe, safe

ALL ABOUT

boredom

Another thing to know about our lives during this pandemic is that many of us are prey to twin monsters. Not *interesting* monsters like the chupacabra, the snallygaster, or old Nessie up in Scotland (if you don't know about them, it's definitely worth a quick Google).

No, we're talking about the twin monsters of Covid-19: BOREDOM and FATIGUE. *Boredom* is when you lack interest or enthusiasm. Boredom is when the things that you used to like don't excite or engage you any more. Boredom is when you feel weary and adrift.

Ennui

An even fancier word for boredom is *ennui*. You pronounce it ON-WEE. If you want to really freak your parents out, we suggest you walk up to them this afternoon and say, "I fear I am succumbing to ennui." Once they get over their shock at how mature and cultured you sound, they will likely roll right into another wave of shock over the feeling you're expressing.

To: Pre-pandemic Self   Details

iMessage with Pandemic Self

Today, 3:43 PM

So, I've been feeling kind of tired 🥱 and bored lately...

Tired?! Have you forgotten how much we use to run around doing stuff? School 🎒 Band Practice 🎼 Soccer ⚽ French Lessons 🥖! We never sat still!

Ok, this is the one thing that has REALLY changed! Basically we stay home 🏠 most of the time. Some of us go to school part time but lots of other stuff has just stopped...OR we do it online 💻

French Lessons Online?! 💻 🧑

Yeah. Honestly, it's hard to keep my eyes open... ⚽

Delivered

Let's finally do that thing where we paint eyeballs onto our eyelids! Then you can sleep and look awake at the same time! 😜

iMessage   😃 ⅰ|ⅰ|ⅰ

But the thing is, everyone is right there with you. We all feel bored at times during this pandemic. For one thing, we're home a lot more - with the same people, the same pets, the same toys, the same games, the same snacks, and the same schedule. Anything that is the same for too long can get boring. Even awesome things like pizza would get boring if that's all you ever ate. Just know that it's ok to feel bored, and that everyone else is feeling bored right along there with you.

Part of feeling bored is feeling *fatigue.* *Fatigue* rhymes with *intrigue,* but it's kind of the opposite. Intrigue conveys excitement - secret plots, daring plans and adventuresome spying. Fatigue is feeling tired, often for no good reason. Skiing all day or raking leaves for hours with your dad often makes you feel tired in a good way. But during a pandemic, when you're doing the same stuff over and over and you're sometimes bored, fatigue doesn't always feel good - it can feel lousy.

Maybe you don't know this, but *lousy* means awful, terrible, abysmal, but it also means...wait for it...infected with lice!? Ha! The English language is so good to us.

◆ ◆ ◆

So, ⸮❓⸮
what can you do about...
⸮❗⸮

boredom, fatigue, and social distancing

When you're feeling overcome by boredom, fatigue, and isolation, the first thing to do is not to ignore your feelings. Your feelings are important. They're letting you know something is off.

Your Feelings Are Important!
Why Not Try...

Reading Poetry
Listening to Music
Taking a Bubble Bath
Writing in a Journal
Reading a Book
Cuddling With Your Pet
Practicing Yoga
Going For A Walk
Chatting with You Friends
Drawing A Picture
Hugging Your Mom
Aromatherapy

Ignoring messages your body is sending you isn't usually a good idea. Remember when you thought you were about to sneeze, but then thought you could control it? Remember when you couldn't hold it in and ended up sneezing on your family's platter of nachos? NOT SO appreciated, was it?...

So, take into account what you're feeling, and then see if you can do something to counter it. The great thing is that you can do things to be less bored, more energetic, and less isolated.

Exercising, for example. Exercising can

make you tired....but it can also make you feel more energetic and awake! It's sort of weird, how exercise can cause a feeling (like tiredness) or the exact opposite of that feeling (like energy). If you've been sitting around with an iPad all day....use exercise to get rid of that fatigue!

Other things can make you feel better, too. Play the piano, get together with a friend for a socially-distanced hangout, eat that last brownie you promised your grandma you wouldn't eat before dinner, challenge your brother to a jump rope contest, see if you can finally run faster than your mom around the block.

just an aside

All these things will help to activate EN-DORPHINS in your brain and will make you feel better. Endorphins are awesome chemicals that live in your brain and are released by exercise. They're like the best sugar rush ever!

◆ ◆ ◆

CHAPTER FOUR
Feeling ALL the Feelings...

"Feelings...Nothing more than feelings..."

These are the actual words to an actual song. We're not kidding. People used to sing this song. Out loud and without shame. In public. On the radio. It was a huge hit.

Wait, what? People still sing about feelings? Ah, yes, "catching feels." But aren't those "feels," ah, how can we put it delicately, a bit different?

You know...a little spicy, but very nice-y?

Well, whether or not you're "catching feels" these days, you're probably feeling something. The pandemic is causing lots of people to feel lots of things - and not all of them are good. Some of them are downright tough - difficult, even. So, let's break them down...

To begin with, more kids are reporting that they're bored, or that they feel isolated from their friends. Some of us are feeling anxious, or are even depressed. The uptick in these types of feelings is not surprising. We're all staying at home and we're all missing our normal routines.

Dear Normal Times, I can't believe how much I miss you. There's just so much that's changed. I miss being able to hug my grandparents. Standing outside in the driveway just isn't the same. I miss being able to go to the movies. My mom says that we may not see a movie in the movie theatre for years. I miss eating in restaurants. If I have to have macaroni and cheese one more time, I think I might actually lose it. I miss being able to go to birthday parties. Zoom birthday parties just aren't the same. That one escape room was kind of fun, but after so much time on screens, I just can't even look at a screen - even if it's for my friend's party. You know what else I miss, I miss my activities. Soccer, doing the play, being in band, going to dance class - I just miss doing stuff. But what I miss most of all is hanging out with my friends. Anyway, Normal Times, if you're out there, we all just really miss you and can't wait for you to come back . XO, Me

Who would have thought that just

being normal would be something we could miss so much...

ALL ABOUT

depression and

anxiety

Do you remember when your grandma got you the crystal growing kit for Christmas? At first, it seemed kind of lame. You thanked her politely, of course, but it wasn't like your favorite gift or anything. Then, one rainy day, you got it out and did it with your dad on the kitchen counter. You followed all the steps, and then watched, waiting for the crystals to instantly grow. Well, it wasn't too impressive that first day. But by the second day, boom! It grew like crazy!

Depression and anxiety are kind of like those crystals. If the right ingredients are there, they're much more likely to grow. That's true for anyone.

Of course, everyone feels sad or worried

sometimes. It would be hard to be a kid during this pandemic without feeling a little sad or worried sometimes! But depression is like feeling *sad plus*. You not only feel sad and tired, but stuff that you usually really like doesn't make you happy anymore. It might also be really hard to concentrate on anything.

Anxiety is like that too. But instead of being about sadness, it's when you worry a lot. Maybe you just can't stop thinking about bad things that could happen, or you can't focus on your schoolwork because you're so worried. Or you can't fall asleep or relax.

The tricky part of these is that everyone feels like this some of the time. Everyone! It's totally normal. But even if you only feel depressed or anxious some of the time, there are things you can do to help yourself feel better.

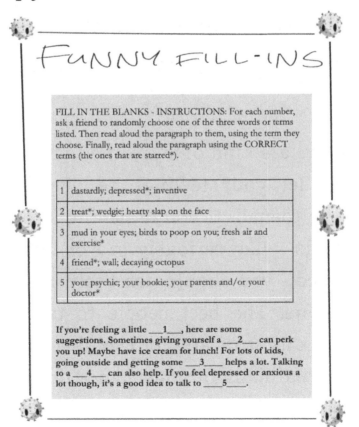

FUNNY FILL-INS

FILL IN THE BLANKS - INSTRUCTIONS: For each number, ask a friend to randomly choose one of the three words or terms listed. Then read aloud the paragraph to them, using the term they choose. Finally, read aloud the paragraph using the CORRECT terms (the ones that are starred*).

1	dastardly; depressed*; inventive
2	treat*; wedgie; hearty slap on the face
3	mud in your eyes; birds to poop on you; fresh air and exercise*
4	friend*; wall; decaying octopus
5	your psychic; your bookie; your parents and/or your doctor*

If you're feeling a little ___1___, here are some suggestions. Sometimes giving yourself a ___2___ can perk you up! Maybe have ice cream for lunch! For lots of kids, going outside and getting some ___3___ helps a lot. Talking to a ___4___ can also help. If you feel depressed or anxious a lot though, it's a good idea to talk to ___5___.

Don't forget that tip about the doctor or therapist! Remember when you had the disgusting, ingrown toenail, and, at first, your mom thought she could fix it at home? Remember how she chased you around the house, how you ended up out on the deck screaming and wailing like a prisoner under extreme duress? After all that drama (and high pitched agony), remember how quickly (and painlessly) the doctor was able to treat it?

Doctors are kind of awesome that way. Don't let your feelings be like that gnarly toenail. If you're having strong feelings - like seriously sad or wildly worried - you should definitely talk to someone. The best people to talk to about this stuff are your adults - parents, guardians, or your doctor or therapist.

Of course, you can also talk to your friends. Remember them? They can help you feel better, and you can help them feel better, too.

just an aside

We're not saying that there are *never* problems with friends. Having problems with other kids is part of growing up, but it can definitely get out of hand. Sometimes, too, problems with friends can get worse if you're only talking online, like during a pandemic. That's where fighting, bullying, and cyber-bullying come into action. For some kids, not seeing your classmates in person might mean that you don't fight with them at all anymore. But for other kids, it might mean that cyberbullying can become a big issue. Bigger even than that septic toenail...

◆ ◆ ◆

All About

people being mean on line

Even if you're not seeing your friends

as much in person, you might be seeing them a lot more online. This can help your feelings, but sometimes it also makes things harder.

That Seems Suspicious....

Crazy, right? How can something that's good also be bad? Well, most things have two sides. Remember how exercise can sometimes make you feel tired, but at other times can make you feel energetic? Screens and friends are sort of like that. Seeing your friends online can make you feel better, except when it doesn't. It can go either way. If you want to tell which way the wind is blowing, well, think about some of these screen-related problems.

First, let's think about a time when seeing friends online is great. Like when you play D&D or Minecraft or Among Us together. Even if you're the Impostor chasing down your friends and killing them, everyone is still having fun. But sometimes seeing other kids online is not so good. Sometimes they can be real mean trolls.

(For those of you who might not know, the trolls we're referring to here are not the adorable ones who dance and sing upbeat songs by Justin Timberlake. Oh no, we're talking about trolls on the Internet, who just live to say mean things online and make fun of others. Definitely not nice behavior...)

just an aside

All this leads us to cyberbullying. Cyberbullying has always been a problem, and we know that it definitely hasn't gone away. If anything, it may have increased due to all the additional screen time.

◆ ◆ ◆

There's no one cause of cyberbullying. It can happen because someone's bullying you at school; because they are mad at you; or even just by accident. You could be cyberbullied about your phone, or the games you play, or pictures you post, or your new mask. It also happens sometimes because it's especially easy for people online to be misunderstood - we bet you can remember a few times when that's happened!

Let's see how much you know!

If you (or your friend) were being targeted online by someone mean, which of the following activities are most likely to make you feel better? There's more than one answer!

If you (or your friend) were being targeted online by someone mean, which of the following activities are most likely to make you feel better? There's more than one answer!

ACTIVITY	YES OR NO
Get a friend, go to a big field together, and run from one end to the other while shrieking your head off. Then smile at each other and do it again.	
Read an article in the *New York Times* about how everyone's super depressed during the pandemic. Blah.	
Talk to your brother or sister (the one you really like) about how you should react or ignore the mean person. Think about cool strategies.	
Turning your typical Family Sunday Dinner into a much more exciting Hot Fudge Sundae Dinner.	

Yes,no,yes,yes

So, ??? what can you do about...

if someone's mean to you online

If someone's bullying you online, it's really tempting to get back at them or to obsessively find out everything they're saying about you. Of course you want to know! Who wouldn't? But if you ask kids who have been targets of cyberbullying, they don't usually talk about how it helped to find that stuff out; instead, they most often talk about how it's sticking with friends that really made them feel better.

So, FaceTime your friends. Message with them. Or even just call them on the phone! Wouldn't that shock them!

Bottom line (and it's a *big bottom*): spending time with friends you love and trust can help you feel better. Not only that, it can help you feel like you don't care so much about a meanie. It can help you feel stronger.

Also, don't forget that you have adults who want to help out. If you're being bullied, talk to an adult you trust. That might be your parent, or a teacher, a school counselor or nurse, or even your doctor. Remember your doctor, of recent (glorious) toenail fame?

Of course, we know that you know that people you know aren't always the problem. Sometimes strangers want to talk online, or other kids who you might have played a game with but have never met. What then?

To: Pre-pandemic Self   Details

iMessage with Pandemic Self
Today, 4:28 PM

> We still have to be careful about who we interact with online...

Yeah, I know about that...

> I know you know! Don't give out personal information - your email, your address 🏠, your full name, Mom's credit card number 💳 ....basically don't give any personal details to strangers online.

C'mon! We've known that since first grade! 😊

Today, 6:45 PM

> Well there was that one time when we gave away our email addresses to get extra lives in that online game 🎮 .... 👾

> Remember that? Remember how many emails we got from that random website? Big Mistake. Huge.

Alright, well, one slip up. We are much more savvy now.. 😎

> It's just more important during a pandemic to be super safe online. Everyone is online all the time! And don't forget that you might feel pretty sire that someone is a really nice person...but you never really know...

Delivered

iMessage   😊 ᵜᵜᵜ

This might seem really repetitive, because we know you've been hearing about Internet safety since you were in diapers. "Be safe online!" your parents said. "Goo-goo!" you agreed. But we needed to bring it up one more time, since everyone is online so much right now. Ok. We know you got it! Time now to move on!

CHAPTER FIVE
what CAN we do?
what SHOULD we do?

O k, so it's a little hard to answer this, because we're in a totally new and totally different kind of situation. We've given you some good ideas - finding a good place in the house to do schoolwork, getting off the screens sometimes, thinking about how you're feeling, getting some exercise and fresh air, and talking to your friends and your family - these are all good ideas. And let's not forget about Hot Fudge Sundae Sunday Dinner!

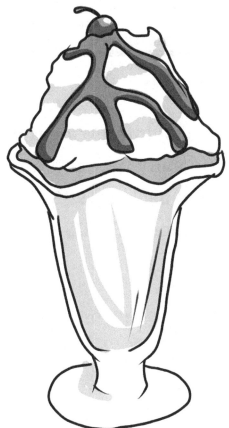

But maybe you're thinking that none of

this might help, because this pandemic is *so completely new.* Except there have been unusual situations before, and, just like now, we didn't all know exactly what to do.

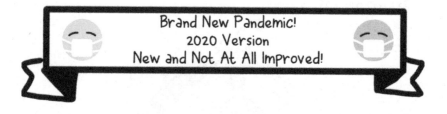

One of the most interesting times when something totally new and unexpected happened was back in 1938 - and it happened right here in the USA.

Of course, as we all know back in 1938 there were still dinosaurs roaming the earth. Ha ha!

Ok, there weren't dinosaurs, but it was practically like the time of the dinosaurs because there was only radio for fun - no internet, no Tik Tok, no YouTube, no Minecraft, and not even television. <le gasp!> Everybody just listened to radio shows, all the time.

◆ ◆ ◆

Anyway, a famous radio personality named Orson Welles decided to make a *fake radio broadcast about Martians landing on the earth in spaceships.* We're not kidding about this. So, he made this show, and even though he told people multiple times during the broadcast that it wasn't real, a lot of people thought it *was* real. Because Martians had never landed a spaceship on Earth before, no one knew what to do!

A lot of people shrieked and ran around. Some hid in their homes. Some dug holes in their backyard to hide in. Some even brought their guns out and started shooting at a local water tower (even though they'd probably seen it every day of their lives). Maybe they thought it was a Martian water tower?

No matter what you think about our current situation,we're sure we can all agree the last thing we want to do is start shooting at water towers. Good, we're glad everyone is on the same page.

While nobody had any idea what to do when they thought Martians were landing, we do have some ideas about what to do during this pandemic.

It's lucky that nowadays we have a lot of really smart experts and scientists and doctors to listen to. That's a huge help! So, while we don't have all the answers, we are learning more everyday.

ALL ABOUT

risks and benefits

The two big ideas that seem to really help the most are RISK and BENEFIT.

Risk is this wire thing you use to mix up eggs. No! Wait. That's a *whisk*, not a *risk*. Ah, yes. Risks are things you could  lose, if you're not careful. Benefits are the stuff you stand to gain.

Let's take a silly example. Let's say you decided to slather yourself from stem to stern in butter in an attempt to beat the Guinness Book of World Records longest Slip-N-Slide in the backyard[2].

This brilliant idea has both *risks* and *benefits*.

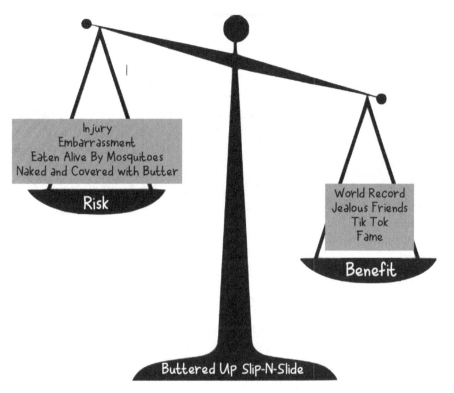

As you can see, there are some RISKS. First, you'd be naked and covered in butter. That sounds risky for a whole host of reasons. You might get eaten alive by mosquitoes. The mosquitoes wouldn't believe their good luck. Somebody took their favorite dish, skinned it, and seasoned it. De-lish!

Then, there's the catastrophic potential for injury. We're thinking skinned knees, but everywhere. And lastly, there's the risk of embarrassment whenever you go trotting around in your birthday suit.

On the other hand, though, there are also BENEFITS. First, there's the glory of that Guinness World Record.

Longest, Buttery
Backyard Slip 'N Slide

Think of the fame, the notoriety, the no-
bility of holding such a record. Think
of how crazy jealous all your school
friends would be. Imagine their shocked
faces as they see your name get blasted
all over the news. What's that worth?
Priceless. Plus, you'd be a star. You'd on
Tik Tok for *sure*. You'd be a viral sensa-
tion...in more ways than one.

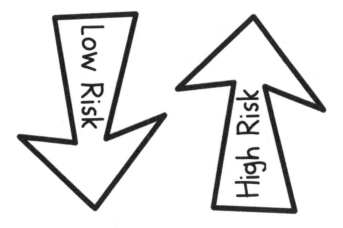

Now that we understand RISKS and BENEFITS, let's apply those terms to our current situation. Each time we consider doing something during the pandemic, we have to consider what we'd gain and what we'd stand to lose.

Let's take something we all want to do - go to see our grandparents, give them hugs, and spend the day inside baking cookies, playing games, and watching movies.

That visit sounds wonderful - there are clearly so many BENEFITS. But, there are also a ton of RISKS.

RISK	BENEFIT
MEDIUM RISK	MEDIUM BENEFIT
LOW RISK	LOW BENEFIT
LOW RISK	MEDIUM (OR EVEN HIGH) BENEFIT

3 Driving by, lowering the window to hold hands
4 Zooming with Grandma
5 Having a meal with Grandma outside - like a picnic, spaced 6 feet apart

Some activities are LOW RISK and HIGH RISK no matter what. Experts tell us that there are three factors to consider when deciding how risky something is - they call them "The Three Cs."

The Three Cs stand for -

Closed Spaces - with poor ventiliation,

Crowded places with many people, and

Close-contact places with close-up con-

versations.

Closed Spaces

Crowded Places

Close Contact

Close Up
Conversation

Closed Spaces - Crowded Places - Close Contact - Close Up Conversation

When any one of these Cs is there, risk
starts to go up. When all three of
the Cs are there, it's always HIGH RISK.
That's called **convergence.** Convergence
is when all three Cs happen at the same

time. Let's think of a silly example. Imagine that your entire extended family really wanted to take a submarine tour. How risky would that be? Well, let's see...submarines are small, closed spaces with no ventilation. With all those family members hugging, chatting, and sneezing, that would be HIGH RISK for sure. Because all the risk factors would be present it would represent **convergence**.

On the other hand, imagine all those family members spread out in a big field for a socially-distant picnic. That would be LOW RISK because people would be outside, spaced at least six feet from each other, with lots of fresh air circulating.

Even your grandparents might be able to join you for that open air get together. Now, wouldn't that be nice?

just an aside

Let's use an analogy as another way of understanding **convergence**. We know your parents will *love* this one!

Consider, if you will, the *three Ss of farting in school.*

1. Sound
2. Stench
3. Surroundings

Let's take the first - **sound**. If you have to pass gas in school, your fervent hope and prayer is that it will be silent. If you can drop a silent air biscuit, then maybe no one will know.

Second - **stench**. You'd also probably hope that if you have to break wind in class then it is of a more delicate aroma.

The last thing you want is everyone in art class making faces under their masks as they sniff your handiwork.

Third, your **surroundings** are key. Are there people around? Darn. Are those people silently taking a spelling test? Double darn.

Unfortunately, if the three Ss *converge*, you could be publicly outed as someone who couldn't hold his meat loaf.

◆ ◆ ◆

Most things don't have total convergence, like riding in crowded elevators for fun. Sure, you know that's a high risk thing to do. That's an easy one! But most risks are harder to judge. There's often no EXACT spot where doing something turns risky.

Please read through these silly elevator-based activities and try to rank them. Keep in mind everything you know about social-distancing, mask wearing, benefits, and risks.

ACTIVITY	Rank the risk High, Medium, or Low
Riding in an elevator by yourself	
Riding in an elevator with Santa and all his reindeer	
Riding in an elevator with 10 people having a wrestle and yodel contest	
Riding in an elevator with your mom	

Low,Medium,High,Low

Now, imagine that you'd eventually like to consider activities that don't involve elevators. With each new variable you add, things can be more tricky to navigate.

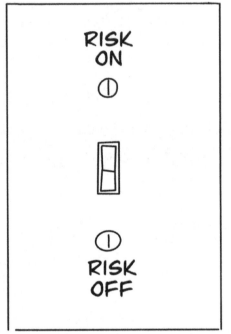

Truthfully, most risk isn't just ON/OFF; it's more like turning on the hot water to take a shower. You turn it a little hotter; then change your mind and make it a little cooler. You have to judge it as you go along.

Safety during a pandemic is like that. Lots of us like sports, dance classes, karate, and other fun activities. Are those safe? Before you play travel soccer or join that paper-making class, you and your family have to decide how much risk you're willing to take on, and how important the benefits are. You have to be flexible and think about all the details, in advance, adjusting as you talk and consider.

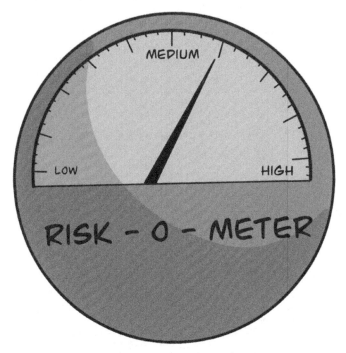

Do you have an older relative living with you? Then you probably need to be safer and more cautious and take FEWER RISKS. Are your parents really healthy, and your grandparents live hours away? Then maybe your family will decide it's ok to take slightly MORE RISKS.

Either way - the most important thing you can do to reduce risk is to *wear your mask*! Decorate it - draw on it - glue beads on it - dye it - but *wear* it!

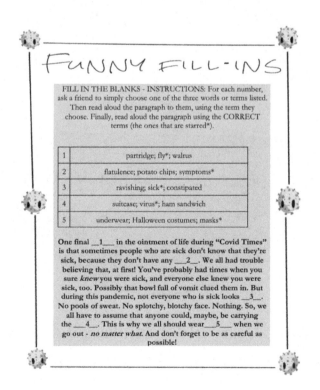

FUNNY FILL-INS

FILL IN THE BLANKS - INSTRUCTIONS: For each number, ask a friend to simply choose one of the three words or terms listed. Then read aloud the paragraph to them, using the term they choose. Finally, read aloud the paragraph using the CORRECT terms (the ones that are starred*).

1	partridge; fly*; walrus
2	flatulence; potato chips; symptoms*
3	ravishing; sick*; constipated
4	suitcase; virus*; ham sandwich
5	underwear; Halloween costumes; masks*

One final __1__ in the ointment of life during "Covid Times" is that sometimes people who are sick don't know that they're sick, because they don't have any __2__. We all had trouble believing that, at first! You've probably had times when you sure *knew* you were sick, and everyone else knew you were sick, too. Possibly that bowl full of vomit clued them in. But during this pandemic, not everyone who is sick looks __3__. No pools of sweat. No splotchy, blotchy face. Nothing. So, we all have to assume that anyone could, maybe, be carrying the __4__. This is why we all should wear __5__ when we go out - *no matter what*. And don't forget to be as careful as possible!

CHAPTER SIX

stuff you can do!

I nterested in thinking more about this pandemic, and how you and the other kids you know are coping with it? Here are a few insanely awesome activities you can try. When you're done, show your family and friends your work. Better yet, do these activities with them - in a safe, socially distanced way, of course!

Write a letter to "Normal Times" and describe three things you DON'T like about life during the pandemic, and three things you DO like.

EXAMPLE

Dear Normal Times,

I don't like not going to school, but I like getting to sleep later!

I don't like not seeing my friends at school, but I like not running around every morning like a crazy person getting ready!

I don't like not getting to hug Granny, but I like all the funny memes she sends me now!

Sincerely,

Me in Not Normal Times

Dear Normal Times,

Sincerely,
Me in Not Normal Times

FUNNY FILL-INS

For each number, ask a friend to randomly choose one of the three words or terms listed. Then read aloud the paragraph to them, using the term they choose. Finally, read aloud the paragraph using the CORRECT terms (the ones that are starred*).

1	your yearly physical; activities*; a trip to the Congo
2	risks*; the latest trends in sneaker-wear; toboggans
3	stinky; highly-dangerous; outdoor*
4	rotund; intelligent; sick*
5	family*; enemies; masseuse
6	cheesecakes; pustules; decisions*

Bottom line, when it comes to planning ___1___ it's important to a) be aware of the __2___ b) consider ___3____, distanced alternatives, c) consider the three Cs, and d) remember that not everyone who is sick looks ___4___. At the end of the day, you might make a pros and cons list and talk about it with your ____5____. You can decide together what is best for you, and know that different families will make different ____6_____ - that's okay.

Create Your Own!

FILL IN THE BLANKS

1. Write a paragraph with 4-5 sentences.

2. Choose the words that you want to be "Fill-In" words.

3. Number the blanks.

4. Create a table with two columns.

   - In Column ONE, put the numbers that correspond to the blanks.

   - In Column TWO, put the correct answers, but also put silly answers.

5. Now play the game with your friends!

Sometimes the best way to keep our own spirits up is to help someone else.

Write down three people, and three things you could do to help them out. Be creative! Here are a few examples.

Mom	Give her a snuggle when she tucks you in at night. Don't go BLECCH when she kisses you.
Grandma	Finally agree to play chess with her online.
Best friend	Make brownies and drop them off.
Elderly neighbor	Ask if they like their walkway shoveled the next time it snows.
Music teacher	Record a video clip of your performing your favorite piece

Try Your Own Risk-Benefit Analysis!

For any activity you're thinking of doing, write down all the Risks and all the Benefits. This will help you decide whether or not you should do it!

RISKS	BENEFITS

How's about some REWARDS!

Nothing can bring focus to school work like the idea of a reward. We know that all our motivation should come from within - we should want to get through that last reading assignment on Epic because we love learning so, so much. But let's be real here. There's no person living who doesn't like a reward. A prize. A small token for working long and working hard. Think about the dentist's office. We should all want to go to the dentist. But we surely do not. And there's nothing more rewarding after sitting through an extremely invasive cleaning, and trying to answer all the hygienist's questions with your mouth both open and closed and saliva streaming freely down your jaw, than not one but **TWO** prizes from the treasure chest. We don't care how old you are, that chest is dope.

School work can be like that, too. It's hard to concentrate. It's tough to tell your brother that no matter how fast a typer he is, he is NOT SUPPOSED to take your typing test for you. But when you're all done (or part way done, at least), it can be wonderful to have something to look forward to. Maybe a system where you get stars and save up for things. Like getting take-out instead of chicken, rice, and corn for the 4,329th time. Or maybe you want to save up for the PS-5.

If that's you, good luck, my friend. We've been waiting six months for just a *desk.* We think the wait time on a PS-5 is at least three years!

Whatever it is that you look forward to, plan on giving yourself little rewards, or treats, or gold stars, or brownies. (If it's a dentist's office treasure chest - more power to you).

challenge!

What are some things you can reward yourself with when you've gotten through your school work for the day? Or, what are some things you can have to look forward to later on?

Write down three rewards you can enjoy today.
Then, write down three long-term treats you can look forward to.

1.	
2.	
3.	
1.	
2.	
3.	

THE INSANELY AWESOME END!

ABOUT THE AUTHOR

Elizabeth Englander, Katharine Covino, & Caroline Charland (Illustrator)

Dr. Elizabeth Englander is a Psychology professor and the founder and Executive Director of the Massachusetts Aggression Reduction Center at Bridgewater State University, a Center that delivers research, resources and programs about social emotional learning and peer relationships. She is a nationally recognized researcher and speaker, and the author of several books and more than a hundred articles.
http://www.elizabethenglander.com

Dr. Katharine Covino is an Assistant Professor of English Studies who teaches writing, literature, and teacher-preparation classes at Fitchburg State University. Her research interests include critical pedagogy, gender, and identity. She has published and presented on issues related to literacy praxis. Prior to teaching at the university level, she taught middle school and high school in Austin, Texas. She is also a children's book author with multiple upcoming projects in the works.

Caroline Charland is an exceptionally talented 12-year-old artist, whose drawings illustrate this book. She is currently in the seventh grade and aspires to become a professional animator.

BOOKS BY THIS AUTHOR

When The Kids Come Back: A Return-To-School Guide After The Covid-19 Pandemic

25 Myths About Bullying And Cyberbullying

Bullying And Cyberbullying: What Every Educator Needs To Know

Understanding Violence

THE INSANELY AWESOME PANDEMIC PLAYBOOK

*Look for the companion
guide to this book:*

The Pandemic Playbook for
Parents and Teachers

Made in the USA
Coppell, TX
09 February 2021